A brief perspective on the local church

Neil Townsend

DEDICATION

D.

ACKNOWLEDGEMENTS

Thanks go to everyone who has helped me along the way, in particular those who have helped me on this booklet: my initial readers Rosie, Steve, and Gareth, and then the proofreaders Lucy and D.

The cover image is by Sergio Souza on unsplash.com

CONTENTS

Introduction   1

A bit of background   3

A local Church …   7

A response   16

Conclusion   20

Appendix: How can that be?   21

INTRODUCTION

This booklet comes out of a casual remark in a burger restaurant in the USA. We were chatting away about something or other when, off the cuff, one of the people I was chatting with said, "You English guys are really loyal to the local church."

And he was right – at least in my case. I am. Yet his words got me thinking: am I right to be so loyal? Was it blind habit or a genuinely biblical belief? So I set out to refresh in my thinking what the bible says about the local church, and bring together what I found in one short summary. This is it! I hope you find it helpful.

A BIT OF BACKGROUND

The word for church

The word that is translated church in the New Testament is the Greek word *ekklesia*.[1] It means a gathering or an assembly: a group of people who have come out of a wider community to gather together. The Faithlife study bible defines it as, "any public assembly or gathering of people in a political, religious, or informal sense". In Jesus' time, therefore, a synagogue was an *ekklesia*.

Not surprisingly, *ekklesia* became the word used in the New Testament to describe a local gathering of believers, a local church. However, it is also used to describe the fact that all Christians are members of the global, universal, and eternal 'body of Christ' which is spiritually one now and will be physically gathered eternally.

The question is, which one is being talked about when? It can be easy to assume that when the New Testament talks about church, it is talking about the second of these: the

---

[1] In the NIV Exhaustive Concordance of 1990, 113 of 114 references to church in the New Testament are from *ekklesia*, the remaining one is from *plethos* (people, group, assembly, number)

universal group of people who are Christians.

"Y'all"

When the bible is translated into English, there is a problem in English which it is hard to avoid: the word 'you'. In most languages, there are different words for when 'you' (and 'your') refers to one person (as one child said to the other: "you are my bestest friend in the whole wide world") and when 'you' refers to many people (as the teacher said to the class after a fight filled playtime: "Class, I am not pleased with you.").

This is a challenge because most of the New Testament was not written to individuals ('you singular'), it was written to 'you plural' – local, gathered, churches.

For example, when Paul says in Colossians 2:6, "Therefore, as you received Christ Jesus the Lord, so walk in him," The 'you' is plural: he is writing to the local, gathered, church in Colossae: encouraging it ("you-plural") to walk in him (singular – Jesus). It doesn't show up easily in English, but the contrast between the plural of "you", and the singular of "him" makes a point.

Remember that when this letter was received in Colossae it would have been read aloud to the whole gathering. It didn't turn up as a mass email to individual email accounts, read by each person on their own, in their own time. No! It arrived as a single letter, read aloud, to everyone gathered together.

The point here is this: the command to walk in Christ is first a command to the group as a whole, as a church, and therefore the individuals in that church. It is to the church explicitly, and the individuals by implication. Not the other way round.

As an experiment, to help explore this, whenever you read a "you" in the New Testament letters, try replacing it with "you all" (or "y'all"), to help remember that it is plural. Most of the time, that will be a more accurate translation.

Ekklesia revisited

The word *ekklesia* was also used in New Testament times for the governmental assembly in each city-state, especially in Greece. It had the final say on all matters governmental – setting laws, electing magistrates, developing and deploying the military, and it elected representatives to the day to day oversight of the running of the city-state.

So when *ekklesia* is used to describe a local gathering, it carries more than the idea of a club, or a religious group. An *Ekklesia* carries the idea of carrying responsibility for and authority over an area. It declares war on enemies, and it welcomes in friends.

Jesus

Jesus only uses the word *ekklesia* directly twice, both times in Matthew.

In Matthew 18:15, he is describing how a member of an *ekklesia* should act if a brother sins against him or her. This passage can only make sense if it is referring to *ekklesia* as a local gathering, what we would call a local church.

In Matthew 16:18, following Peter's declaration of Jesus as the Messiah, Jesus says this, "… I will build my church (*ekklesia*), and the gates of hell shall not prevail against it."

Given his use of *ekklesia* in Matthew 18, and the common use of the word *ekklesia* to mean a local gathering, Jesus is talking about the local, gathered, church (the "religious" sense of *ekklesia*) – and its mandate to push back unwanted evil (the authority and power sense of an *ekklesia*). [2]

---

[2] This is one reason why church planting and growth are major spiritual battles: the gates of hell seek to oppose local church precisely because it is created, called, and empowered to overcome darkness and take ground.

An illustration

Hindsight allows us to understand that the universal church is included in Jesus' statement in Matthew 16. So how does that fit together?

In 2018, the football world cup was held. In the final, the French team and the Croatian team played each other, and the French team won 4-2.[3] Or, to put it another way, France won the 2018 World Cup. If you had spoken to a French person after that match, they will have proudly declared, "we won".

Somehow, for a moment in time, those few players *are* the entire nation. They don't just represent the nation, they aren't just the footballing elite of France, they *are* the nation.

Even more so (and unlimited by time), a local church isn't simply a representative of the universal church, it isn't a part of the universal church, it *is* the universal church. Jesus starts with the local church.

All of the fullness of God is in Christ:[4] Jesus is fully God. Although Jesus is one of the trinity, there is nothing of God which is "God but not Jesus". In the same way, the local church is all of the fullness of the church.

Indeed, to put it another way: we understand the universal church by fully understanding the remarkable nature of the local church, not the other way round.

---

[3] *Allez les bleus*, as they say in France.
[4] Colossians 1:19

A LOCAL CHURCH …

So, let us reread some passages from the bible about the *ekklesia* and think about what thry mean.

… *belongs to Jesus*

Matthew 16:17

The emphasis is strong: I will build my church. Jesus is passionate about this thing we call the local church: she belongs to him. Jesus is utterly submitted to the will of the father, yet he sticks his neck out here: the local church is his. He is proud of her, after all, she …

… *is the bride of Christ*

2 Corinthians 11:2

When a man marries a woman, every bit of her is beautiful to him. So is the church, yes the local church, to Jesus. With all her incompleteness, imperfections, variations and blemishes, she is beautiful to Jesus: She is his bride and he loves her with passionate abandon. It perhaps easier to think of Jesus loving the universal church. But Jesus clearly loves the *ekklesia*: the local gathering. The real, everyday, gathering of men and women who are his. He loves that gathering - she is his bride.

And she is quite some bride, as she ...

... pushes back the gates of Hell

Matthew 16:18

Jesus sees a prevailing local church which is pushing back the gates of hell: it is hell that is stormed, not a church that is protected. The local church is the means by which hell is relentlessly pushed back. By every person saved by the gospel, by every person loved into life changing transformation, by every act of righteousness, by every prayer for local government, by every local initiative for the glory of Christ, by every proclamation of the gospel, by every expression of the glory of Christ, by every prayer offered in the market place ... the local church pushes back the gates of hell.

... is the body of Christ

Ephesians 1:22-23; Colossians 1:18,24[5]

As we step more into the New Testament letters, remember that just about every letter in the New Testament was written to a local church and would be read out loud to the gathered local church. Imagine that you are there, in Ephesus, listening as the letter from Paul is read to you: "And God placed everything under his feet and appointed him to be head over everything for the *ekklesia, which is his body ...*" (NIV, with *ekklesia*)

As listeners, gathered together, you would hear that you, the gathering of believers in Ephesus, the local church, *are* the body of Christ. How encouraging to hear this powerful truth.

This is explicitly clear in Colossians 1:24 where straight after saying that he, Paul, is suffering for them (plural, the local

---

[5] There is also a strong case for including 1 Corinthians 12:27 here: "Now you-plural ..." (the *ekklesia* of Corinth) are the body of Christ.

church in Colossae), he says that his suffering is for the body of Christ, his church. The local church is the body of Christ.

And so, when we speak of the local church, we speak of the body of Christ. Paul is deeply concerned about divisiveness in the local church[6] not only because it is destructive, but because it is directly destructive of Jesus' body.

Whatever we do to, and do for, the local church we do to and for the body of Jesus. This elevates our worship and our service to a magnificent, beautiful endeavour. And it challenges us to always live honourably towards the church and those who are the church − those everyday, not-quite-perfect-yet, men and women who are the local church.

As an aside, much as the trinity is both clear (One God, Father, Son and Holy Spirit), and mysterious (how can that be?), how the *ekklesia* can be the body of Christ and the bride of Christ is beyond human intellect.[7]

... *has Jesus as her head*

Ephesians 5:23-24; Colossians 1:18

Perhaps obvious, but worth stating: Jesus is the head of the church. The church, the local *ekkesia*, submits to him.

... *is the family of God*

Romans 8:16-17; Galatians 3:26; Hebrews 2:10-18;

It is repeatedly stated in the New Testament that when we become Christians, we have become children of God. It would be unimaginable to the readers of, and listeners to, these letters that a local gathering, full of the sons and daughters of God, the perfect father, would not be a family. The local church is the family of God.

Family operates at many scales: nuclear, extended, and

---

[6] *eg.* Titus 3:10

[7] Or mine, anyway.

wider! The local church is part of the universal family of God. But it is clearly, absolutely, family of God in its own right.

The only question is: what kind of family do we make it?

... is saved by Jesus

Ephesians 5:23

This might seem like an obvious point, but it is quite profound. We understand that Jesus' death and resurrection worked forgiveness for our sins and reconciliation for us (as individuals) with God. That Jesus is also the saviour of the church means that the divisions between humans that stopped them forming healthy societies and groups has been forgiven and that reconciliation is possible at a group as well as at an individual level. And the church is the model of this.

When Jesus speaks about the church revealing the wisdom of God, one of the most profound ways the church does this is because the church, as a local body, can live in the power of Jesus as saviour for all of the church members collectively. The church can live and model reconciliation at the group level. It is designed to be a bringer of unity not only between individuals, but also between groups. Jesus died for that.

... is the temple of the Holy Spirit

1 Corinthians 3:16

While in 1 Corinthians 6:19 Paul specifically says that the bodies of individual Christians are temples of the Holy Spirit, here he emphasizes that the group of people he is writing to, a local church is, collectively, God's temple: you-plural yourselves-plural are God's temple and God's spirit dwells in your-plural midst.

Holy Spirit, loves to dwell in you and me as individuals, as daughters and sons of the most high. He also dwells in the collective entity that is a local church. The local church isn't simply a collection of individual temples of God. It is, itself, a temple. This is one reason why corporate worship, corporate prayer, corporate action, corporate welcoming of Holy Spirit, corporate preaching, corporate outreach (and so on) matter so much. There is a temple of the gathered which is distinct and special (just as the temple that is each individual believer is distinct and special).

... *has an angel held by the Lord*
Revelation 1:12-20

Revelation contains an epic vision which John had. In this early part of it he sees a vision of the Lord (1:13-15) who was holding seven stars in his right hand (1:16). Those stars are the angels (or messengers) of the seven churches (1:20).

There are seven stars, not one, not hundreds. Just before these verses, in verse 11, John is given a specific list of seven churches to which he should write. Seven churches (rather than five, or ten), is significant: seven is the number of perfection and totality. They represent each and every local church, as a distinct entity. There are then seven stars. The implication is clear: each and every local church has a messenger, or angel, in God's right hand.

To hold something in ones right hand is a clear picture of authority, of being close to the heart of someone. (It's why James and John wanted to sit at Jesus' right hand in Mark 10:35-44.)

Therefore, each local church, as a distinct entity, is close to the heart of Jesus. Each local church has a direct messenger, angelic access to Jesus' authority, to his right hand. Jesus has a direct line, a specific angel, to each local church. This means that we can have faith that a local church can hear God's voice, follow his call, exercise his authority in a way that is distinct from, special and unique to them and different in scope from an individual believer.

... *makes the manifest wisdom of God known*

Ephesians 3:10

This verse demonstrates that a clear and distinct part of God's intent was that the *ekklesia* would make known the manifest wisdom of God.

Wisdom can be summarised as the art of combining knowledge and understanding to live truly well, from God's perspective. The church: the local church, is created to be a visible demonstration of how God thinks life is well lived. Yes, in individual live, but also as a group. It is the local church which demonstrates that alignment with God means a diverse people can be one body. It is the local church that demonstrates that many, many, imperfect people can be radically transformed for the better, sometimes fast, sometimes over time! It is the local church which demonstrates that compassion, care, justice, and vision can co-exist harmoniously. And so on!

... *is loved by Christ her as his bride*

Ephesians 5:24-29

Paul put together two pictures in verses 25-29. The first picture is of a marriage: just as a (right thinking!) husband loves his wife (passionately, with abandon, to the exclusion of all others), so Christ love the *ekklesia*. Secondly, as the *ekklesia* is also his body he cares for it and feeds it.

In verse 24, just before those pictures, Paul talks of the *ekklesia* submitting to Christ. The universal church does submit to Christ, but that submission only actually happens, is only truly worked out, when a local church seeks to live and act in submission to Christ. So when Paul goes on to talk about Christ loving the church, he must have the local church in mind.

It applies to each local church: Christ loves her. He loves

the local, gathered, church, and delights to care for her. He loves your local church with passion, and cares for her, and provides for her.

.. is Christ

Acts 9:4-6; Philippians 3:6

In Acts 9, Saul encounters Jesus dramatically on the road to Damascus.[8] In that encounter, Jesus says to Saul, "Why do you persecute me?" This must have been confounding to Saul: he had been persecuting the church in Jerusalem and he was on his way to persecute the local church in Damascus (Philippians 3:6). So Saul asks, "Who are you, Lord?". "I am Jesus, whom you are persecuting," comes the reply. There can be no other conclusion than that Jesus identifies so closely with the local church, in Jerusalem, in Damascus, anywhere, that Jesus considers it to be himself.

To be clear: Jesus considers that persecuting the *ekklesia* is to persecute him. Touch a local church (for good or ill), and you get as close to touching a tangible Jesus as you can, this side of heaven.

... is the house of God

1 Timothy 3:14-15

Paul is writing to Timothy, who has been left bringing leadership to the local church in Ephesus (1 Timothy 1:3). Here Paul expresses his hope to visit this local church, while acknowledging that he may be delayed. Yet Paul is confident that the people who make up that church will know how to behave "in God's household, which is the church of the living God." The background and the context show that Paul was referring to the local church in Ephesus as "God's household".

---

[8] This is the Saul who would be renamed Paul in the coming times.

A household, in those times, would be a large group – the father of the household, his wife, their children and extended family, and the servants. Given all the other descriptions of the church and believers in the New Testament, this one fits perfectly: the local church is where God is at home: with his family.

The local church is where the presence of the father is most regularly encountered, and where the family gathers for family events: at great times of celebration, and at moments of challenge, and simply for the regular rhythm of family life. God is active everywhere, at all times, and can be met everywhere, at all times. But home, his home on earth, is the local church.

... is the pillar and foundation (bulwark) of the truth

1 Timothy 3:14-15

Continuing in the same passage, not only is the local church where God is at home, it is the pillar and foundation of the truth. In John 14:8 Jesus declares that he, Jesus, is "the way and the truth and the life." Not surprisingly, given all that is laid out above, the *ekklesia* is therefore the means by which that truth is affirmed, and held in the right position.

Wherever there are people, a local church is needed to ensure that truth is held on to. Local church is what repeats, endorses, communicates and calls people to truth. Gospel truth, yes; God's truth, yes; but also simply the power and inestimable quality of being true, of truth, and of truthfulness.

The very nature of the fall means that people and societies can easily drift from esteeming truth, and from being true. The church, the body of Christ, the household of God, is the antidote to this drift – on the ground, locally.

... was what Paul served and suffered for

Colossians 1:24-25

The New Testament includes some of Paul's letters. It's

instructive to note that, of Paul's letters in the bible, all except one are either to local churches or about leading local churches. Only one concerns an individual's affairs. When Paul calls himself a servant of the church in Colossians 1:25, he must therefore be referring to local churches. In verse 24 he has spoken of suffering for the local church in Colossae.

Paul travelled the (known to him) world, he spent hours with individuals and groups, he was an apostle to and servant of Jesus Christ (Romans 1:1; Ephesians 1:1)[9]. He planted and nurtured churches. Here in Colossians we see how, for Paul, those things drew together into one thing: he was a servant of the *ekklesia*, the body of Christ, the local church. His planting of, his service towards and his suffering for local churches was the core outworking of his call. It was central how he lived out the call of Jesus his saviour.

Why else would he return to groups of people he had led to faith in Jesus, except to encourage them, and to strengthen local churches by appointing elders in Acts 14:21-23, or to require Titus to "put what remained into order" (Titus 1:5) by doing the same?

Paul loved, and served, real, tangible, touchable, local churches.

---

[9] As well as 1 Corinthians 1:1; 2 Corinthians 1:1; Galatians 1:1; Philippians 1:1 …

A RESPONSE

It is very clear that the local church is held in high esteem in the bible. Even though the local church is a gathering of imperfect people with all their not-perfect-yet-ness, even though it may not always feel like everything written above, the local church is of profound importance and value to the New Testament.

To be clear, no local church is yet perfect. Each one remains an imperfect representation of Jesus. Some might even seem to us less perfect than others. Yet that is not the point.

As we have seen above, the bible presents a vast and powerful view of the *ekklesia*, of how God sees the local church and what he strongly desires it to be and to become. So how do we respond to this high call in the reality of actual local church life? What choices can we make about the local church – even our local church?

Love the local church

I love my wife and my children. They are amazing, incredible, created by God filled with amazing gifts, wonderful personalities, and beautifulness. Are they perfect? No. Have they been known (rarely of course!) to do wrong things which leave me bemused or confused? Yes.

Yet I love them, passionately. Sometimes that love flows naturally, and sometimes that love is a choice. A choice to forgive, a choice to love, a choice to bear with, a choice to delight in. A wonderful, life giving, choice.

I choose also to love the local church. I choose to love her for all the reasons above, and not least simply because Jesus loves her. To Jesus she is a beautiful bride walking down the aisle about to marry him for eternity, the one he longs for with every fibre of his being. So I love the local church, sometimes naturally, sometimes by choice, always passionately.

Forgive the local church

One of the first things that goes with love is forgiveness. Without a doubt, if you are part of a group of people, someone will do something, or something will happen, that isn't right from where you stand. You get hurt. Jesus spoke about this in Matthew 18 – there is a clear way for things to be handled. Even so, sometimes, things don't work out, and someone, many people perhaps, end up hurt.

This isn't the place for a full discussion on the importance of forgiveness. The key point is that forgiving the person or group who caused the hurt is a profoundly important key to walking free from that hurt. Just as Jesus has forgiven us. (It's also true for groups – forgiving those groups which have hurt us, just as we are forgiven by Jesus.)

Serve and build the local church

Whilst 1 Corinthians 14:12 calls us to excel in the gifts that build up the church; 1 Corinthians 14:5 gives a clear example: "The one who prophesies is greater than the one who speaks in tongues, unless someone interprets, so that the church may be built up."[10] Elsewhere in the chapter Paul commends speaking in tongues highly, and points out that it builds up the speaker. Building up the individual in the faith is good, but building up the local church is better!

So choose to be part of a local church and seek to use your gifts for the growth and development of that church. When the church gathers, be there, and be part of making it amazing. The best way to be a part of it, to feel connected with it, is to have life giving relationships with other Christians in your church. And the foundation for that to happen is to be there when it meets.

You have God given gifts that can serve, grow, strengthen, build, enhance, extend a local church. Use them for her good. Choose to invest those gifts, not least your money and time, in the local church. Most churches I know could double or more their impact for good, their impact for Jesus, very simply: if every person who gathered to them regularly tithed their money and gave their time to that church's vision, strategy and call. Let's do the greater good and build our local church together.

Honour the local church

Speak well of your church, speak well of other local churches. If the local church is the body of Christ, to speak ill of her is to speak ill of Jesus' body. How can I speak ill of my saviour's body?

To put it another way, the local church is the visible family of God, as 1 John is keen to emphasize.[11] 1 John 4:20-21 puts

---

[10] These verses are in a section of the letter talking about local church gatherings, so again Paul must have had the local church in mind.

[11] For example, see how 1 John 2:7-14 uses family terms repeatedly.

it in stark terms: failure to love our sisters and brothers is a failure to love God. And love expresses itself by speaking well of people.

So, speak well of your church and those in it, not least those exercising leadership in one way or another. Speak well of other churches and those in them, not least those exercising leadership in them. After all, Jesus tell us that by observing our love for one another the world will know that we are his disciples.

Part of this is choosing to trust and follow leaders. I've had the privilege of meeting many leaders of churches. One of the things that they all share is a deep desire to do the best they can for the church they lead. They know that they are imperfect, and make mistakes. Just about every leader I've met grieves over the mistakes they've made, mourns the relationships they've damaged (just about always unintentionally), and prays for wisdom to do better in the future. If there is a sin or an offence issue, please do follow Matthew 18:15 with them.

So please, speak well of, honour, the local church.

Ask for God's help

The local church is a high call. God does seem to call us to challenging things, perhaps so that we won't try and do it in our own strength. Yet he has the strength, the power, and the joy for us to live in these ways, so let's ask him for them!

CONCLUSION

The local church is a big deal: the bible presents us with a powerful, beautiful, glorious, vision of the local church. The invitation to us is to pursue it, in faith, by the grace and power of God.

APPENDIX: HOW CAN THAT BE?

Reading through all the points in this booklet can raise the odd logical issue. The two most common are probably:

How can every local church be all the amazing things you've listed?

As a Christian, I am a child of God, redeemed, transformed, empowered by the Holy Spirit. I am forgiven and set free from sin, and called to do greater works than Jesus. I am empowered to live righteously, peacefully and joyfully in every moment.

Day by day, however, it happens that I don't attain the fullness of each of these. For example, I know only too well the irrational emotions that can well up and threaten me at unwanted moments.

Yet in Christ I am still all of those things. I am forgiven, set free from sin, and so on. The call is on me to seek God, to pursue his forgiveness, welcome his power and to grow into who I already am in Christ.

It is the same with the local church: the bible presents us with a vision of the local church that is full to bursting with wonderful things. The invitation to us is to pursue those things, in faith, by the grace and power of God.

How can something be Christ, the body of Christ, and the bride of Christ?

One of the most profound and powerful doctrines of Christianity is the nature of Jesus: alone of everyone who walked the face of this earth he was both 100% human and 100% God. No human has ever been able to fully explain "how that works", yet it is profoundly true, and important that it was so.

So, in many ways, it should come as no surprise that the local church, Jesus' body, is also a combination of things that, humanly, logically, we can't quite "fit together".

Each of these aspects of the local church should capture our imagination and passion, and it is good to delight in them, and indeed to meditate on them. This side of heaven, they may not quite fit together inside our brains, but God is OK with that, and he invites us to welcome the enormity of his view of the church with wonder and faith.

ABOUT THE AUTHOR

Neil leads Wantage Community Church in the UK and the OpenGate group of churches, which are part of the Salt and Light network, and is part of the international team for The Turning. He is passionate about churches seeing transformation for the better in every person and situation around them. He is married to D, and they have three daughters (and two cats).

abriefperspective@gmail.com

Printed in Great Britain
by Amazon